AGILE BY DESIGN

An inclusive methodology for enterprises that want the best of Design Thinking and Agile

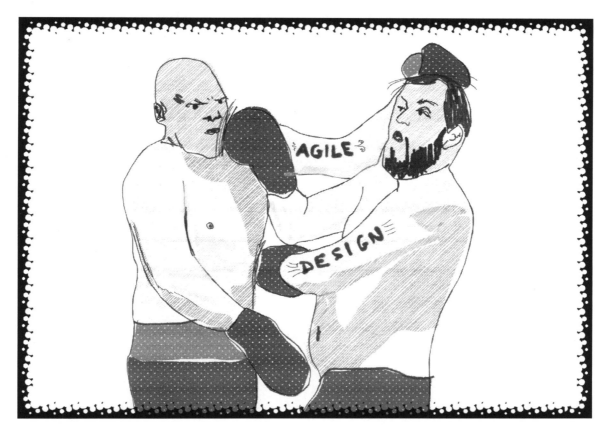

Jai Shankar Vishwakarma

TABLE OF
CONTENTS

ITS ALL ABOUT CHANGE **STRATEGIC VISION** 1
Strategic Vision and Outcome 2
Let's get them in a room 3

DEFINE PHASE: 12

ANALYZE PHASE: 16
People Analysis 20
Process Analysis: 23
Technology Analysis: 26
Agile Readiness Assessment: 27

DESIGN PHASE 35
AGILE by Design 38
Process Design: 43
People & Capabilities: 44

IMPLEMENT PHASE: 47

SCRUM Overview (Roles & Rituals) 50
External Benchmarking for Maturity Model: 60
Communication Strategy: 61
Technology Mapping: 61
Process Management: 62
Project Plan: 64

GOVERNANCE PROCESS: 66

ITS ALL ABOUT CHANGE
STRATEGIC VISION

Every new beginning is messy, and we understand that at the end all of it turns to be good. The beauty of Change is such. While all modern enterprises are chasing the elixir of being a world class service provider, oh well rather it has changed to be a product centric organization, all of them are struggling to be agile, and adopting Design Thinking in its true form. So, let us first start from the strategic direction of the organization, as we all know, unless there is an intent to change, nothing else moves. My work here will act as a field guide for all of you practitioners and ambitious IT consultants, designers, product managers, and consultants; into the world of designing an organization that has embraced design thinking and Agile in its best possible combination however all aligned to the specific direction and vision from the organization's who's who. This work is focused around an organization with some of the most common issues:

- **People** – *The factory model for technology streams failed miserably due to de motivated employees*
- **Processes** – *No definite structure and redundant processes, which are quite waterfall friendly and against agile's core concepts.*
- **Data/Communication** – *No management touch with the ground of developers, again the distance of actual workforce from the strategic vision*
- **Technology/DevOps/CI/CD** – *The technology did not support the overall agility for the developers, and product development.*

Hence the approach that I took might not be what your organization might need, however the methodology remains the same, and can be used for your specific change needs, and organization re design.

Henceforth the approach and methodology should be used at the sole discretion of the reader and pick parts or whole of the methodology for the best fitment within your organization's change.

STRATEGIC VISION AND OUTCOME

The Change Management Approach, like any other good work, has to be established and formal approval in place before we shake a leg. Here's an example of what I put together for the change, which was carefully crafted to cover people, process, technology and communication.

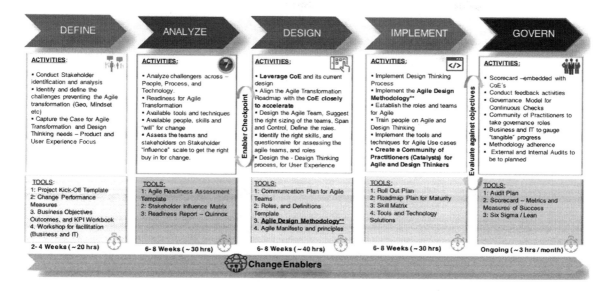

Key assumptions that readers should note are:

- *Approach was focused and its success lied in the way we change people, and influence the cultural gaps that need be to addressed for change to be positive.*
- *Organization re design is not permanent hence the exercise is intended to be carried out again to ensure best is in practice.*
- *The organization had an IT Factory Model in place*
- *CoE existed which was established with an intent to drive innovation*
- *Technology to drive agility did not exist*

LET'S GET THEM IN A ROOM

The first step for the change to take place is to identify and capture the business outcome.

Let's start with identifying the key players and stakeholders who would help you identify the key challenges and help you identify and define the problem, and the future state outcome expected.

Leverage SIPOC approach to conduct enabler workshops that produce information needed to create deliverables that establish a target state Operating Model for Agile + Design Thinking

- *Create SIPOC for the entire Change Management to target the different "variables"*
- *Identify gaps/pain-points in the current set up (IT Factory Model – People, Process, Information and Technology)*
- *Identify issues and future requirements*
- *Identify the roles involved with the exchange of the service (not the role(s) who produced the service)*
- *Discuss, where possible, potential or desired Target Operating Model (Governance and Operations with CoE)*

The information gathered above will be used to:

- *Update Alignment Matrices capturing current and future state TOM (Target Operating Model) content*
- *Update Heat maps clarifying processes in scope*
- *Identify and define the challenges preventing the Agile transformation (Geo, Mindset etc)*
- *Inform future creation of current and target Process and Service models for IT Factory in terms of Agility and Speed to Market (Rapid Prototyping, and Frequent Fast Failures)*
- *Come up/Define a Maturity Model for the IT Factory, identify and define the Change Performance Measures ; Business Objectives Outcomes, and KPI Workbook*

Expectations that should be addressed:

Key Questions around the current state of the IT factory with respect to the Agile Culture:

- *What is the "problem statement", and how deep and wide is it? (Enterprise Layers)?*
- *What to do? (safeguards and improve from here on)*
- *Where we will head? (Road map and TOM)*
- *How will we achieve it? (Methodology, Dissemination/Cross Pollination, and Tools)*
- *How will we measure it? (KPI, Measure, and Objectives)*
- *What will be the alignment with overall "Corporate" or "Business" Goal and Objective?*

Participants at the workshop:

FUNCTION	SME (Subject matter expert)
IT	NAME
HR	NAME
FINANCE	NAME
INFOSEC	NAME
OPERATIONS	NAME
APPLICATIONS	NAME
INFORMATION	NAME
COMMUNICATION	NAME

The overall process for the workshop is as below:

Brainstorm on People, Process, Technology and Information challenges

Used Post-ITs to capture immediate findings, and write the findings on them

Aligned the Post-ITs to relevant "buckets" – People, Process, Technology, or Information Challenges

Rationalized the findings to remove the "duplicate" pain points in the "buckets"

Refined the findings to "vital few", and grouped further

Documented the "Outcomes" and "Objectives" along the way

Identified what would be the KPIs for Outcomes, and the measures

While the process was churning, we were able to identify primarily the people dimension, and communication (data and information) plane as came out to be the top areas of focus.

Below are some of the images captured, and what they translated into:

People – Pain Points being rationalized along with Process, and Technology
(Yellow Post-ITs here are People, Green for Process and Pink ones represent Technology)

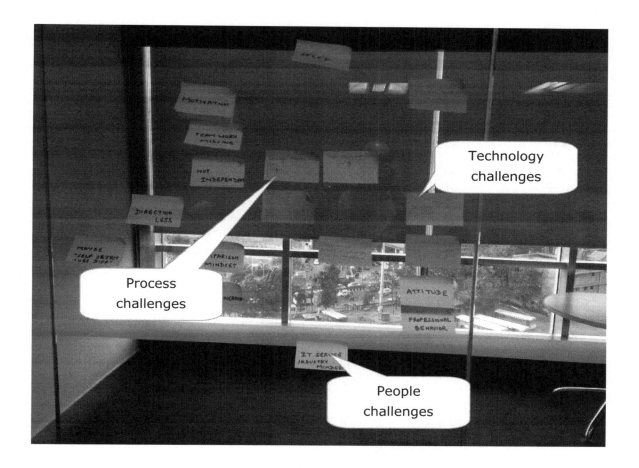

Outcomes and Objectives being deciphered, and elaborated as we come to the final stages of the workshop
(Post-ITs being used to map to the outcomes we expect of the IT Factory)

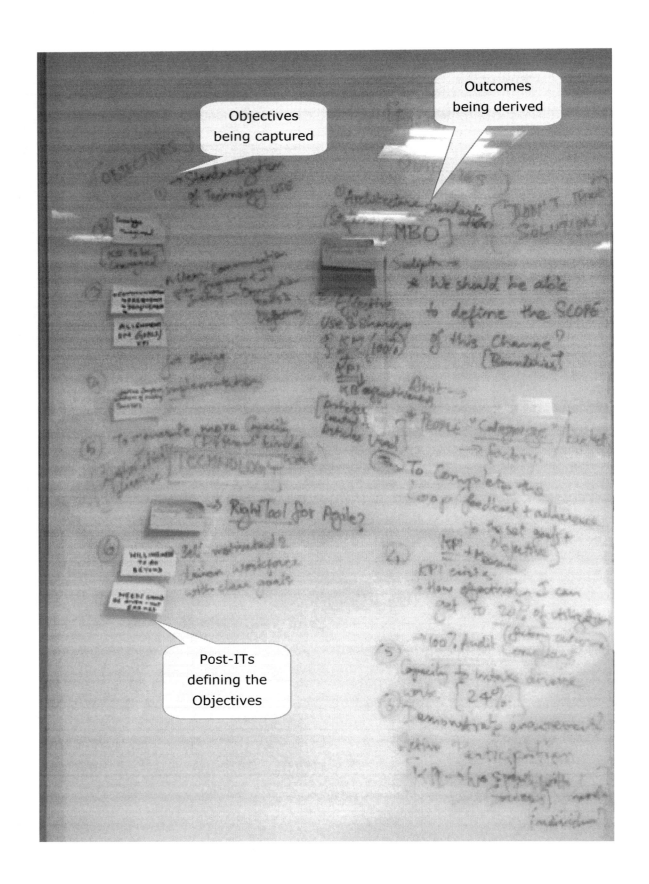

Further refinement of the Outcomes and Objectives:

Some of the Post-ITs that were used to establish the Objectives and Outcomes are detailed below with the context and its understanding:

Standardization of Technology Use –

Business Outcome	Business Objective
BO01 - Architecture Standardization & Re use of artefacts (Ras, Technology Standards – 100%)	OB01 - Standardization of Technology Use

Knowledge Management – This Post-IT refers to the need for a solution that enables effective knowledge creation, re use of the same, dissemination and availability of the Information when needed.
It was understood that there are elaborate Knowledge Bases where videos and articles are expected to be leveraged, and use to be captured, and measured for effectiveness. Which has led to a gap where in the effectiveness was not reported back to the management. (loop back to management to update on the way the KB has been used, and whether it was effective in solving a known issue)

Business Outcome	Business Objective
BO02 - Effective Use & Sharing of KM solution (100%)	OB02 - Leverage KB, Articles and Videos

Alignment of Goals (KPI) – This Post-IT was put in place with the other one – Communication – which was accepted that IT Factory needs to have a communication plan and a frequency set for the same to disseminate the information around the refreshed or otherwise goals and KPI (Key Performance Indicators) for the IT Factory overall, which will then be used to define further the way forward for various initiatives and innovation pipelines, and be realized via following the right Agile pattern.

Business Outcome	Business Objective
BO03 - Adherence to the set goals and objectives (100%)	OB03 - Communication Plan for IT factory

Effective Implementation of existing Processes – Here we referred to the current implementation of the processes, where there seems to be some gaps. This has been captured, and the objective has been defined to ensure bring 100% compliance to the effective implementation and practice of any and all processes as put in place, defined, and metrics to be used to measure the same.

Business Outcome	Business Objective
BO04 - How effectively can I get to 20% utilization (IT Factory)	OB04 - Effective implementation of existing processes

Willingness to go beyond + Needs should be earned not given – These Post-ITs spell out one of the core problems being faced by Factory today which is around a "self-driven" workforce and its power to bring in the right change. Currently this seems to be sitting at the core of all the concerns that the management intends to address. Here the intent of the objective is to get people to have general discussions with the management around what they have as an idea and innovate on making life easy for the rest of the factory. And idea can be anything that has value for the end user. The Outcome is to bring the individuals out of their current mindset to only focus on what they have at hand as "job" to think beyond and get to a level where they can take on new ideas, and suggest how to "improve those jobs" and create pro-active solutions.

Business Outcome	Business Objective
BO06 - Demonstrate Active Participation (hrs spent with Manager on brainstorming)	OB06 – Self- motivated & driven workforce with clear goals

NOW WHAT?

The understanding of the current situation and being able to capture the outcomes and objective is quite important, but what next.

Well, you now know the problem, and that is half the battle won.

Let's now dive into the whole process and start getting serious about the implementation plan.

DEFINE PHASE:

As noted earlier Define phase is all about going deep into the problems and quantifying in the best possible ways to understand the challenges that can further be analyzed.

DEFINE

ACTIVITIES:

- Conduct Stakeholder identification and analysis
- Identify and define the challenges preventing the Agile transformation (Geo, Mindset etc)
- Capture the Case for Agile Transformation and Design Thinking needs – Product and User Experience Focus

TOOLS:
1: Project Kick-Off Template
2: Change Performance Measures
3. Business Objectives Outcomes, and KPI Workbook
4. Workshop for facilitation (Business and IT)

2- 4 Weeks (~20 hrs)

During this phase as you can refer to the image above we will:

- *Identify the stakeholders who would be impacted and would need to be part of the change. Here stakeholders are all parties including managers and employees.*
- *At a micro level identify the challenges across what is preventing the change.*
- *Develop artefacts and tools that can be re used when refresh is conducted.*

As for everything else we need to set the objectives of the Define phase as in the below image:

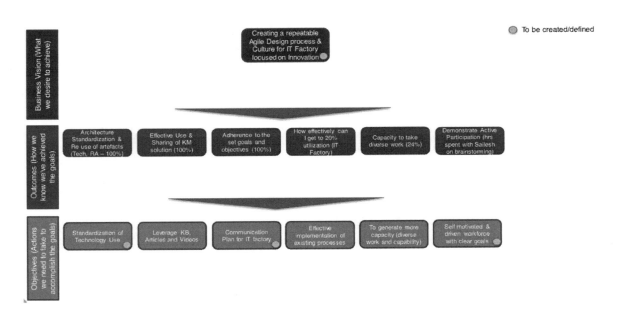

At this stage we also set the roadmap together with the management on what is expected at the end of the change exercise and by when:

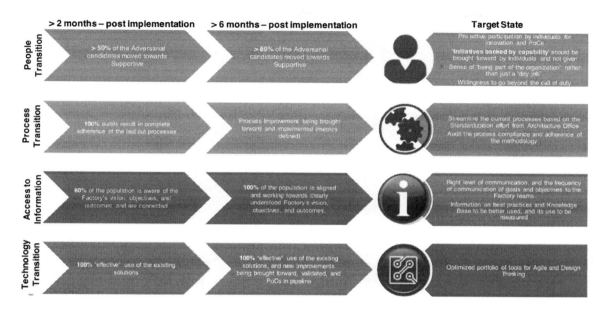

It is quite important to note and document the target state because then you know what you would like to achieve, and it's better to know the future right?

Once we have been able to establish the define phase and its outcome, we then need to get down and huddle in to start analyzing what would we need to do, and also how do we get there.

ANALYZE PHASE:

This phase is dedicated to all the people who like to crunch data and are in love with numbers.

At this stage we need to start with two important aspects:

a) Is the organization/enterprise ready for change, and if yes, what is it that we need to focus on?
b) What is the delta/gap in terms of the outcomes, and objectives defined to what the current stage of enterprise is?

ANALYZE

ACTIVITIES:

- Analyze challengers across – People, Process, and Technology.
- Readiness for Agile Transformation
- Available tools and techniques
- Available people, skills and "will" for change
- Assess the teams and stakeholders on Stakeholder "influence" scale to get the right buy in for change.

Enabler Checkpoint

TOOLS:
1: Agile Readiness Assessment Template
2: Stakeholder Influence Matrix
3: Readiness Report – Quinnox

6- 8 Weeks (~30 hrs)

In terms of the timeline, we anticipate around 6 – 8 weeks of number crunching and analysis of the data that we have to start to understand as this will be detrimental in playing the game of getting the right change in place.

As indicated earlier in the define phase, we will continue to focus on people, process, technology and information likewise to ensure that we get the best of all the four pillars of change needs.

Here we first started with analyzing people in terms of their will and capability to be the "influencers" of change and who would be the first change agents to receive the flame of change we intend to propagate across the organization.

We start with the Stakeholder Analysis, an age old but quite a must exercise that helps us understand people across different profiles.

Agile transformation is not just a "methodology" adoption, it needs a culture change.

Change in itself is quite uncomfortable for anyone. To give you a feel imagine if someone suddenly asks you to scribble some lines using your left hand, where in you have been a right-handed person your whole life. Yeah! exactly that feeling is what we are talking about change effects.

So let's get to the analysis phase but before anything else we need to ensure that we identify the domains that we will assess the enterprise's readiness for change, and the gap for change, which will direct our focus on.

One of the reference materials that you can definitely use for such an assessment is the study from OVUM.

So, here's the factors we considered, in all nine of them to check our organization in study for the Agile readiness, and culture change:

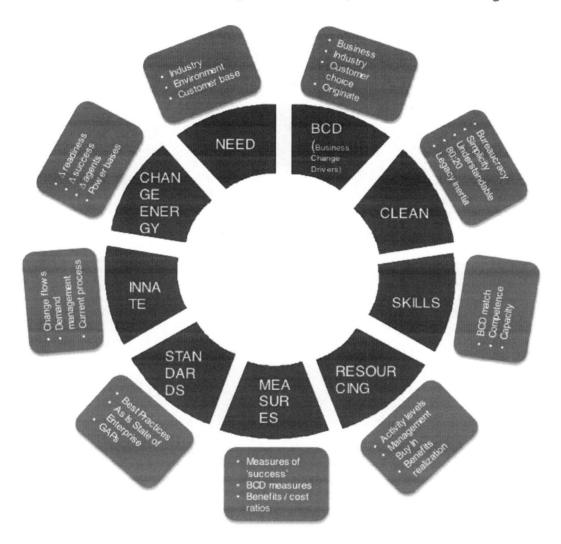

Based on the outcomes that we derive post analyzing these nine factors, will we come face to face with the feasibility of the organizational change that we have set out to achieve.

Let's start with the stakeholder analysis.

PEOPLE ANALYSIS

We interviewed every individual, and yes you read it right, we did call in every individual for a 1:1 meet up, where we questioned them in an informal setting around very precise dimensions to gauge them around power, influence, interest and attitude towards their job.

This was a very important exercise as there needs to be a focus on investing time and resources on people who would really help you achieve your target state, and Zen.

There were two critical statistics that should be of interest to you.

First one as below image is what we used to filter out the people who really are the ones who would hold the flame of change and help us get there, from the ones whom we need to really push and get it done.

Supportive:

This is where our change agents reside and who can "pollinate" the energy and motivation with right levers in place. We need to identify the individuals and give them the support needed to help the cause.

Adversarial:

These are threats to the team, and change, and would need to be paid special attention to get them along the way. Change Agents would be a good lot to cross pollinate here if needed

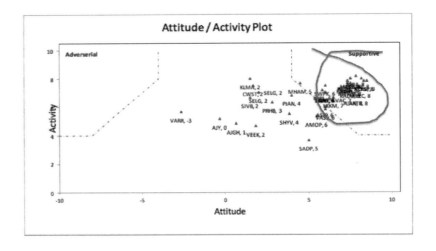

The green zone as in the image above, showcases the people/group that we can get things done with. As for the ones between the red dotes lines are the ones that are the ones we need to focus on for getting in line and attention to be playing part in the change.

The next statistics, focuses on the aspect of the influencers and the so-called power centers within the organizations.

Vital:

This section showcases the key individuals who are indirect power centers within the factory, and show a high interest as well in decision making.

Everything else:

The data points, below the red line showcases the individuals who have passive interest in the factory, and are not influential towards the people attitude change.

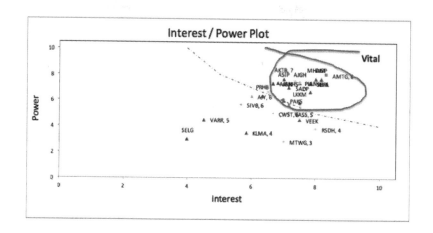

The image above reflects the key group of people who despite of the organizational hierarchy are in a way influencer, and power centers in a way where people get influenced by them offline, irrespective the reporting managers. This graph is quite useful to play with as this helps in understanding who to keep happy and on your side of the game so ensure the culture change is well received and is easy to transition.

Some of the key outcomes of the stakeholder analysis are below.

The images below in sequence indicate and guide us towards what would be the ideal way of communication/information dissemination.

INFORM — **Low Power/influence and High Interest**

This group is very often one of the most critical in the project. It is typically made up of staff at the 'coal face' who feel their day to day jobs are most impacted by the project and the associated change. Ineffective communication to this group may result in them viewing the project as a threat to their jobs, and this will create significant issues later in the project.

INFORM — **Suggested Communication Strategy**

- An open project platform such as a SharePoint site for stakeholders to view the status of the project and possibly participate in discussion or submit FAQs
- Feedback or suggestion boxes (online or physical)
- Anonymous surveys
- Focus groups with key representatives
- Meetings and/or webinars
- Regular all staff update emails
- All staff forums

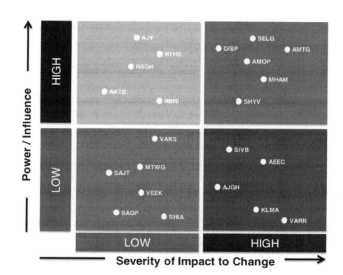

Low Power/influence and Low Interest

This group of stakeholders are the most commonly forgotten, but they very often have an impact later on when the program or system is being implemented. They need to be kept informed about what's going on, and provided with forums to provide input and feedback. That way, if they are interested in communicating something back to you, they will be able to do so and you can deal with it proactively

Suggested Communication Strategy

- An open project platform such as a SharePoint site for stakeholders to view the status of the project and possibly participate in discussion or submit FAQs
- Feedback or suggestion boxes (online or physical)
- Anonymous survey
- The best way to manage this group is through regular 'light' communications

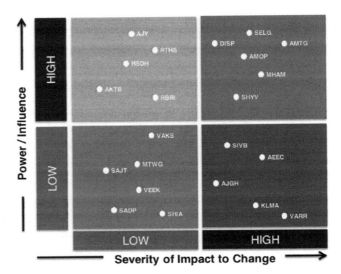

High Power/influence and Low Interest

Typical members of the "Satisfy" group are managers of the organisation. They might not be directly impacted by the implementation of the project, but they have influence in the business and they will care about the end result and the impact particularly in their area. If they start to feel that their area will be impacted, their level of interest will escalate immediately. A good project manager will foresee this and communicate with them before someone else does

Suggested Communication Strategy

- Steering/Advisory/Reference Groups run every quarter or 6 months
- Distributed minutes
- Access to project information webpage with regular updates and impacts
- Keep them satisfied by including them in high level meetings (not too frequent) – **quite possibly they won't turn up, that's OK**, ensure they are sent the minutes and if something does begin to concern them they will know that this meeting exists and the invitation is always open for them to attend

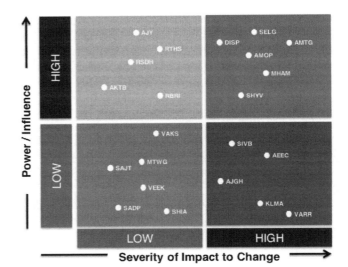

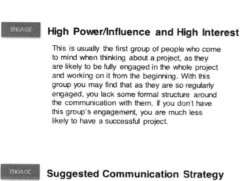

High Power/Influence and High Interest

This is usually the first group of people who come to mind when thinking about a project, as they are likely to be fully engaged in the whole project and working on it from the beginning. With this group you may find that as they are so regularly engaged, you lack some formal structure around the communication with them. If you don't have this group's engagement, you are much less likely to have a successful project.

Suggested Communication Strategy
- A SharePoint site for stakeholders to view the status of the project and have input on discussion
- Working Groups
- Project team Meetings and webinars
- Progress updates

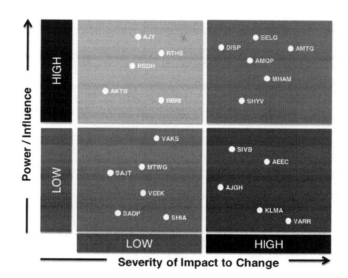

PROCESS ANALYSIS:

Next we focused on the value stream mapping of the existing processes to map the gap / identify needs of the target process.

Here's a quick snapshot of the existing processes we had in place:

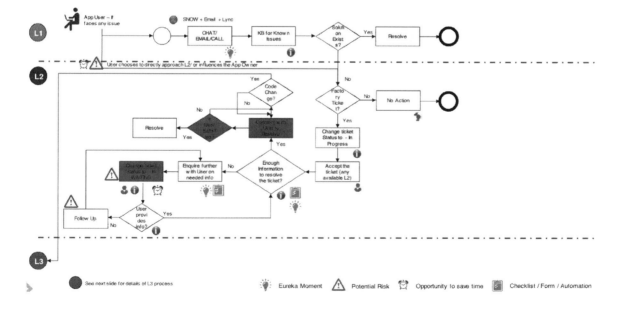

23

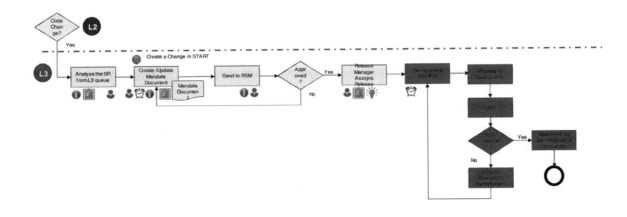

The above images reflect what was the process before we optimized the processes for the organization's objectives and goals.

The process shows the then Application Maintenance and Application Development Factory process that the enterprise was operating around.

We spent some time to identify what would be the waste in the value stream and helped them shape a new process landscape, while identifying automation needs as well, as a byproduct.

The problem for the SAP factory was also the same, and was quite people dependent.

Please see the image below:

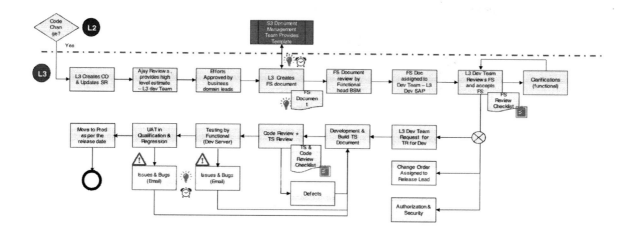

We will show the optimized designs of the process while we illustrate and explain the implement and design phases further down the book.

TECHNOLOGY ANALYSIS:

Next in terms technology, that is the easy part, where we interviewed stakeholders, and did an on ground assessment to see what processes are technology enabled, and what were the technologies that helped in the eco system of Agile readiness. The below image showcases the process and tools/applications overlay that helped in the agile/ culture change.

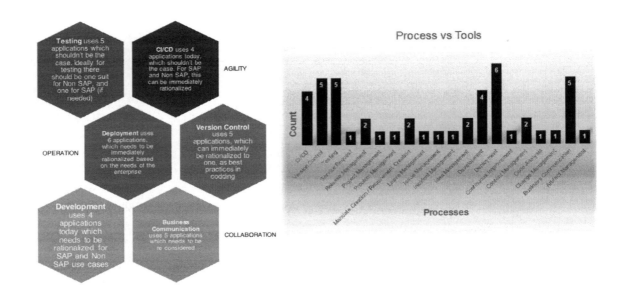

AGILE READINESS ASSESSMENT:

Let us now elaborate on all the factors of the Agile readiness assessment that we illustrated above (the nine factors), and share with you what we assess and what was the look of the ideal.

Here's the detail on the nine dimensions and its definition:

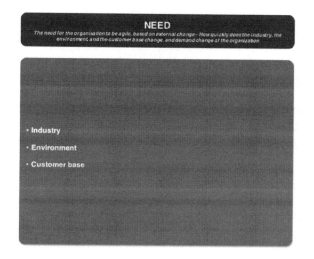

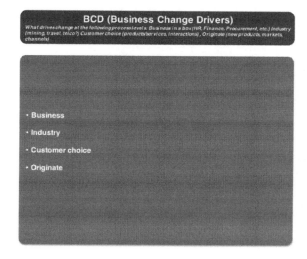

CLEAN

How 'clean' is the organisation: Bureaucracy load, business simplicity, understood processes, activities, environment, 80:20 mind-set, legacy inertia

- Bureaucracy
- Simplicity
- Understandable
- 80:20
- Legacy inertia

SKILLS

Does the organisation have skills that match the BCD model? What are the competence levels, what capacity levels? Skills apply to both business and IT

- BCD match
- Competence
- Capacity

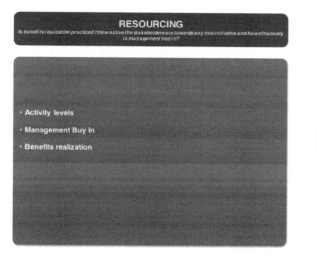

STANDARDS
What is the adoption of best practices, and trend setting standards at the organization, and how well is the change adoption for past programs?

- Best Practices
- As Is State of Enterprise (use of tools, processes, and mindset)
- GAPs

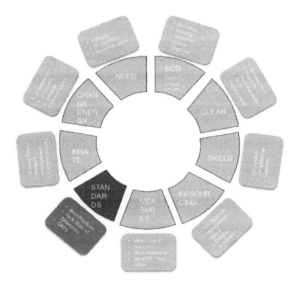

INNATE
How innate is change in the organisation? How does change flow / get blocked? How is demand managed?

- Change flows
- Demand management
- Current processes

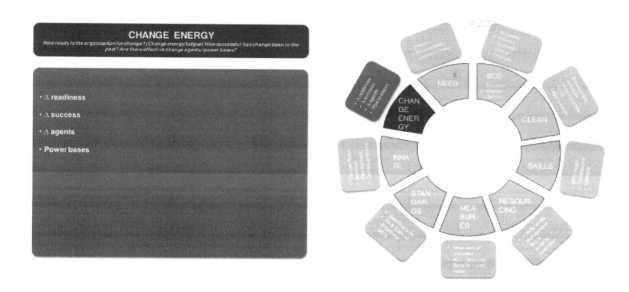

The above images are self-explanatory where we defined the factors and the aspects we would use to measure the organization's readiness for change.

Do note that this is a **CULTURE Change**, and the earlier you realize that it's not just about people, process, technology and information, but it's about the whole picture.

Also to help you guide on the sample of the factors and its maturity, here's a matrix you can use for your organization's assessment:

		1	2	3	4	5
Need	How quickly does the environment in which your industry / sector operates change	Virtually no change. The industry changes within a static environment. No external pressures on the industry to change	Low level of operating environment change. Some legislation, or environmental change.	Medium level of environment change. Every year some change or legislation occurs that forces an industry response	High level of change in the environment. Fast changing, evolving legislation, or environment change forces many annual changes on the industry	Intense change. Often difficult to keep up with what is changing / has changed. Need constant industry response. Need constant environmental monitoring
	How fast changing is your industry / sector	Virtually no change in this industry / sector. Things stay the same from year to year	Low level of change. Some changes occur annually, without much pressure to keep up.	Medium level of change. Some industry processes / methods / products change on an annual basis	High level of change. Most methods / products / processes have some form of change in a year	Intense change. Industry processes, products, methods constantly changing
Business Change Drivers	How often do your customers / suppliers change	Our customer / supplier base is a constant. Very little change demanded from them	Every now and then our customers or suppliers require us to change our products / services or channels	We need to make changes on an annual basis to accommodate customer / supplier change demand	Our customers or suppliers change regularly, requiring us to change as well	There is constant change in our customer / supplier base, requiring on-going change to our products / services / channels
	How often are basic business rules / processes / practices required to change	Almost never. We seldom change our basic business practices (HR, Finance, Admin, Procurement, Legal)	Low level of change. Occasionally we change basic business processes and rules.	We change our some of business rules / processes / methods every year	Our basic business rules / processes / methods change often. There may be a backlog	We are constantly changing our rules / processes / methods. There is pent-up demand to change the basics
	How often do you need to change the industry practices / methods that you use	This is a very stable industry. We seldom change the way we conduct industry specific methods / practices (E.g. Mining, Healthcare	We make occasional changes to the way we work in our industry practices	Every year we change at least one major process / activity to keep up with industry trends	We change numerous industry practices / processes and methods to keep ahead of industry practices and standards	We constantly change our practices and processes. Our industry approach is in a state of flux. We see ourselves as ahead of the game.

And here's an example of the way you can calculate or assess the maturity:

Level	Description
1	Factor does not exist, or is extremely immature. Very low scale.
2	Low maturity / low representation / low value. Factor tends to be accommodated on an ad hoc basis (Sometimes / some place). Some understanding of need.
3	Moderately mature. Factor may be patchily represented, or have incomplete implementation. However the intention is there and is proven.
4	Mostly mature, with some outliers. Usually documented / practiced. High scale.
5	Factor fully mature. Strategically inculcated. Full governance. "The way we do things here"

Here's a visual representation of the final statistics on what was the final readiness assessment via a simple spider chart:

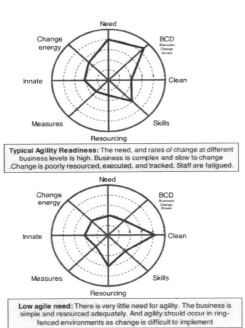

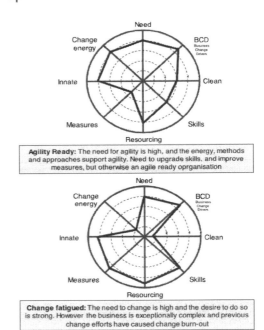

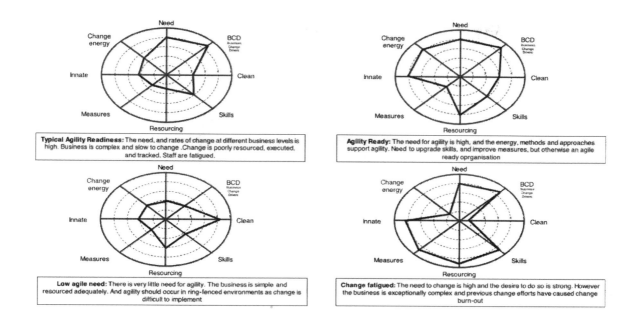

All of the above graphs, represent a typical (guide) on where this organization is in terms of readiness for agile across the nine dimensions of change.

Once we have analyzed the factors and have a very good understanding of people intent, stakeholders affluency, process gaps, technology plane and the most important result – agile readiness assessment report which will now help you design a new operating model and organization.

Let's now put some throttle and start with the design phase which is quite critical, because this is where we are now going to use all the data that we have at our disposal for the right mix of the organization.

Something that you must continue to note that the entire change / organization design is focused around the objectives and goals that we have defined during our first phase of this change exercise.

In addition to the Analysis of factors one of the most important aspects is to understand the journey of the people, process, technology and the way the organization is constructed today. Customer journey mapping is of immense importance to ensure you are capturing the pain points and in the right areas.

Here's what we managed to capture:

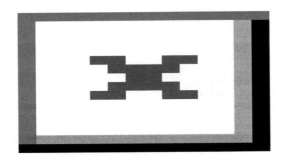

We definitely see that the current processes and the way factory was operating was neither making the end users happy nor were the developers in their zone of comfort.

DESIGN PHASE

This phase is quite critical in nature as you would now have to use your experiential knowledge, data collected from the analyze phase, and all the information collected, shared from different stakeholders to start shaping a new organization that will meet the target state's needs.

DESIGN

ACTIVITIES:

- **Leverage CoE** and its current design
- Align the Agile Transformation Roadmap with the **CoE closely to accelerate**
- Design the Agile Team, Suggest the right sizing of the teams, Span and Control, Define the roles.
- Identify the right skills, and questionnaire for assessing the agile teams, and roles
- Design the - Design Thinking process, for User Experience

TOOLS:
1: Communication Plan for Agile Teams
2: Roles, and Definitions Template
3. **Agile by Design Methodology****
4. Agile Manifesto and principles

6- 8 Weeks (~40 hrs)

This phase comprehends all the necessary information collected and analyzed in the previous phases to create a new design for the enterprise that can bring the best of Design Thinking and Agile in practice.

However, before we design the target operating model we should establish a clear guidance for the design. The image below is what we recommended and used in our case for organizational transformation:

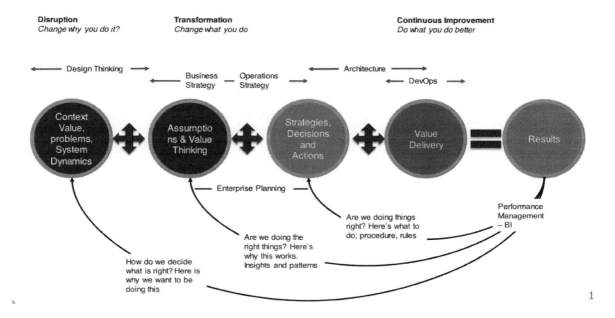

The key factors to consider are:

- Change why you do it
- Change what you do
- Do what you do better

Additionally, the components that we addressed were strategy shouldn't be on white boards but there has to be an implementation to it and a KPI or Outcome driven approach to know what is going upwards or otherwise.

Based on the above premise, here's a series of diagrams that will help you understand what we cam out with.

I have christened it as "**Agile by Design**". The very reason as it takes a very different approach to Agility and is focused towards a product centric, intrapreneurship approach, that can help build faster, assess faster, re work faster and ship faster.

---

[1] Source: Enterprise Architects

AGILE BY DESIGN

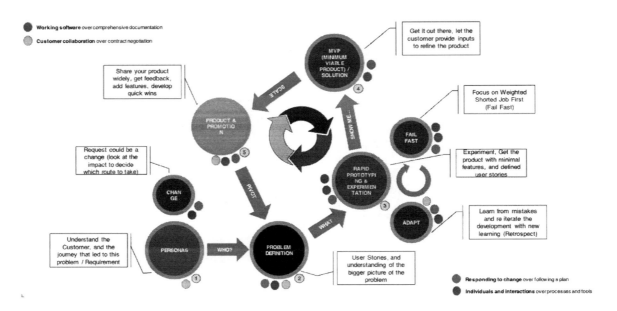

Key things to observe would be that we have taken the principles of Agile very seriously, adapted Lean startup concepts and merged the context of Design Thinking together.

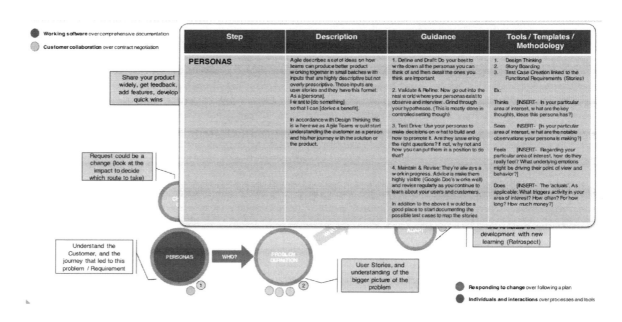

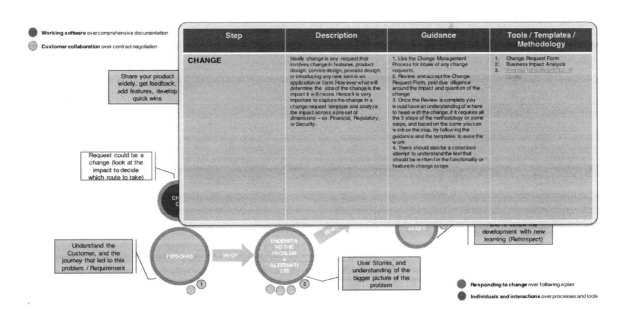

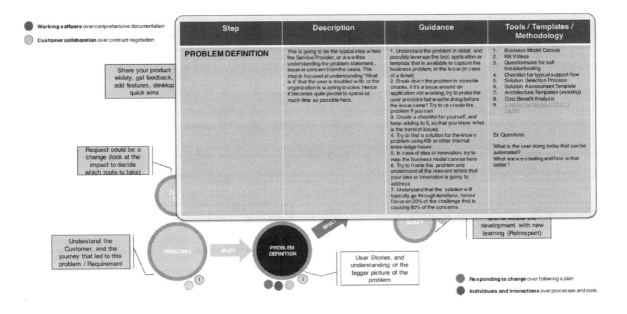

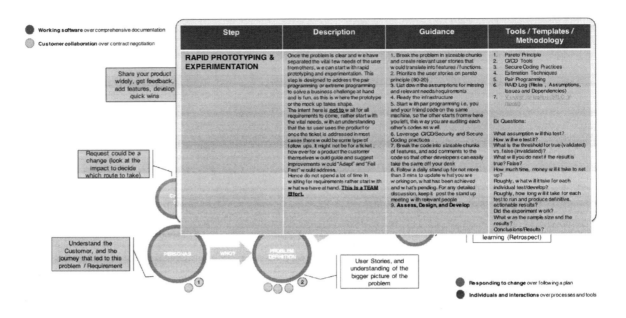

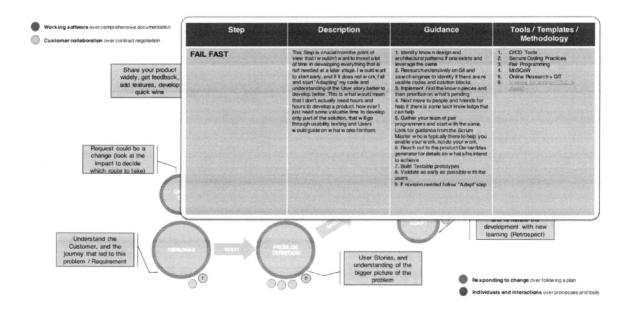

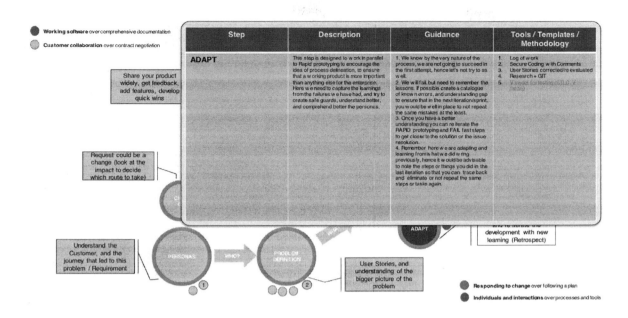

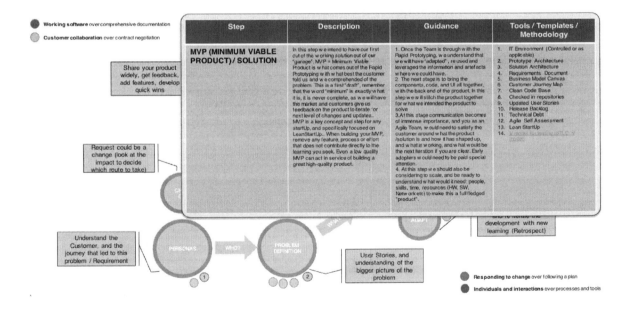

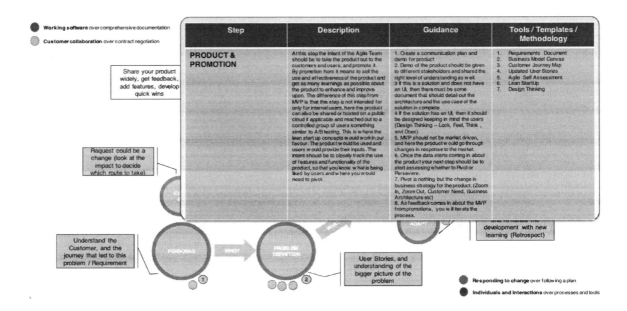

The above stages and steps are self-explanatory, however to guide you to an extent of implementation, please pay attention to the Table in the pictures.

The way its illustrated is, to show case what the name of the step is, what is the description of the step, what is the guidance for the step, and what would be the tool, technology solutions or methodologies in the market that you can use to accomplish the steps.

We hence state that this work is not about endorsing any company, tool or technology but is agnostic of these, it's a repeatable methodology that you can use to accomplish an organizational change where you are addressing a major shift in culture.

Agile by Design is possible only when we set a target state for ourselves, and define the outcome to ensure that once we see these changes, we can say that we were successful.

The below image is one such example that we used.

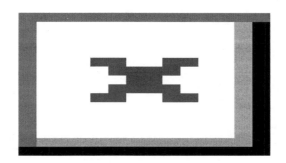

Next in design we need to establish the Agile process, of SCRUM in perspective to the organization. Since this is a Factory model of Application Maintenance and Application Development we chose SCRUM to be an ideal choice.

PROCESS DESIGN:

Here's what the To Be state of process looks like:

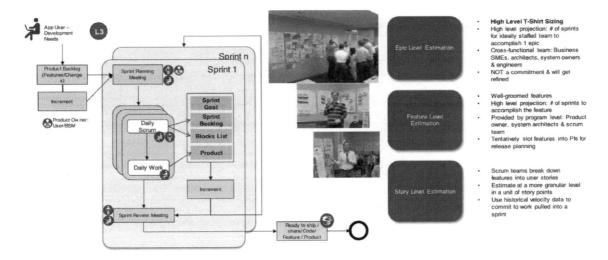

We introduced a couple of transformations to the ideal SCRUM process, like product backlog refinement which in this case open or historical issues, and their prioritization.

Next, we made one choice SCRUM for both SAP based business functions and non-SAP practices as well.

It's is pertinent to now elicit the roles, their descriptions and the processes/rituals that the teams and individuals have to live in. Here's a snapshot of the same:

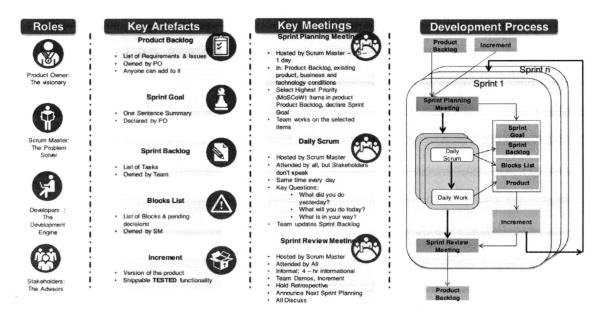

PEOPLE & CAPABILITIES:

Next in terms of the JDs (Job Descriptions) you will have to define for each of the roles you are introducing here, to ensure that there is alignment of the Agile concepts to the enterprise.

An example of what we did is here:

Roles and Responsibilities for Agile and Scrum Projects

Project Title	[type the project title here]	
Project Manager		
Document Version & Change History & Update Date		

Title	Role	Name
Product Owner	Provides product strategy, vision and direction for the project. Responsible for creating and maintaining a Product Roadmap that brings an (MVP) minimum viable product, application or service to market in an iterative fashion. As "the voice of the people" the Product Owner represents the End-User & Customer, and is liaison between this community and the Agile/Scrum Development team, working closely with both groups to ensure there is clear understanding of what features need to be in the product, application or service and what priority order those "feature sets" need to be implemented. The Product Owner is continually involved, including defining the project and actively reviewing the progress.	(Name of Individual)

Responsibilities

- Defines the features of the product and translates these into "User Stories" that are I.N.V.E.S.T. (Independent; Negotiable; Valuable; Estimate(able); Small; Testable
- Responsible for maintaining and grooming the "Product Backlog" (evaluating, planning, strategizing & prioritizing User Stories)
- Drives User/Sponsor/Customer Feed-back loop that directly affects the Product Backlog priority
- At least quarterly, determines product release date(s), milestones and content that align to vision and Product Roadmap
- Key participant and contributor to Sprint Planning process
- Responsible for the profitability of the product (ROI)
- Responsible for prioritizing features according to market and perceived customer value
- Adjusts product features and priority as needed after each sprint, iteration, or every 30 days, as needed
- Accepts or Rejects work results
- Participates in "Daily Scrum" meetings and assists to clarify any details as they are developing (PO may provide a surrogate representative)
- Responsible for leading the "Sprint Review" which takes place at the end of each development Sprint.
- May be a part of the Scrum Development Team, however will not also assume the role as Scrum Master

Once we have designed the target model of operations, let's now try and bell the cat. Implement phase is where all the magic happens.

IMPLEMENT PHASE:

This phase focuses on the most sensitive part of any organizational change, which is how do we do it?

We planned a phases approach to implementation. And this is where planning and strategy is so important. We had already identified the stakeholders, identified the gaps in the processes, roles need, and the technology needs. In the implement phase we try and stitch it all together.

IMPLEMENT

ACTIVITIES:

- Implement Design Thinking Process
- Implement the **Agile Design Methodology****
- Establish the roles and teams for Agile
- Train people on Agile and Design Thinking
- Implement the tools and techniques for Agile Use cases
- **Create a Community of Practitioners (Catalysts) for Agile and Design Thinkers**

TOOLS:
1: Roll Out Plan
2: Roadmap Plan for Maturity
3: Skill Matrix
4: Tools and Technology Solutions

6- 8 Weeks (~30 hrs)

We start with the ground work we had started with stakeholder analysis.

We first lay out a clear plan for roll out.

For your understanding here's what we did for employees. Note that this is not a one-way street. This culture change cannot be done alone by the ground up, there has to be a top down approach to engage the customers/clients in a manner that we meet at the same cross road, and move ahead in union.

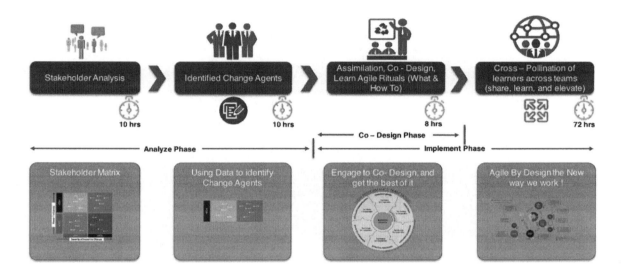

Next, we invite the customers:

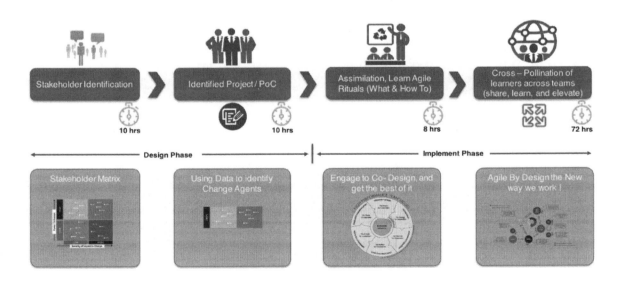

SCRUM OVERVIEW (ROLES & RITUALS)

Let us also define the different roles that will now be introduced to the enterprise:

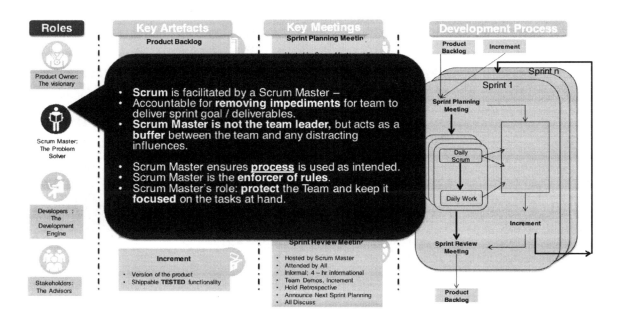

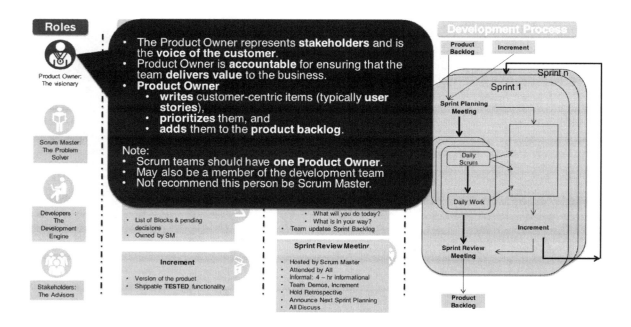

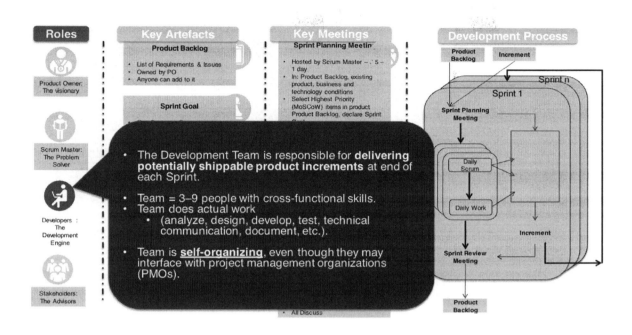

Next, we discuss on the key artefacts that would be produced by the Agile teams and will be used to move things forward.

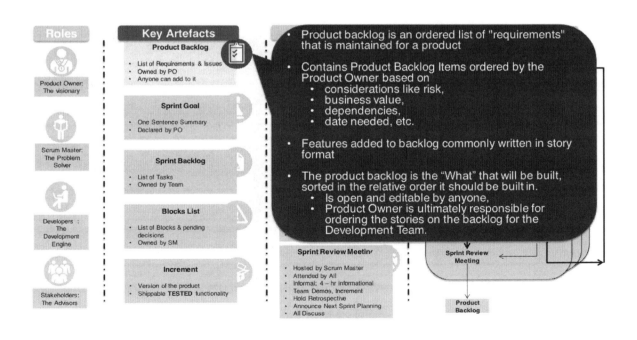

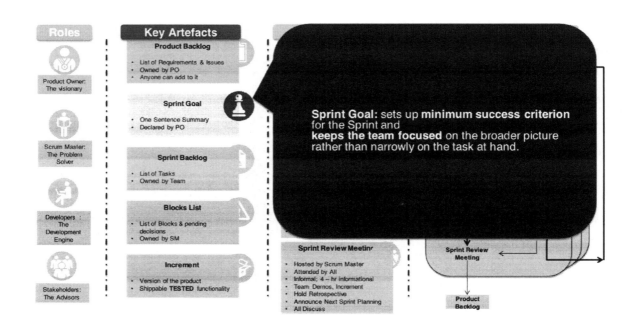
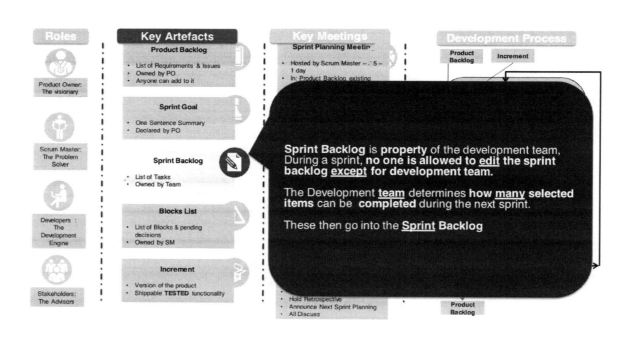

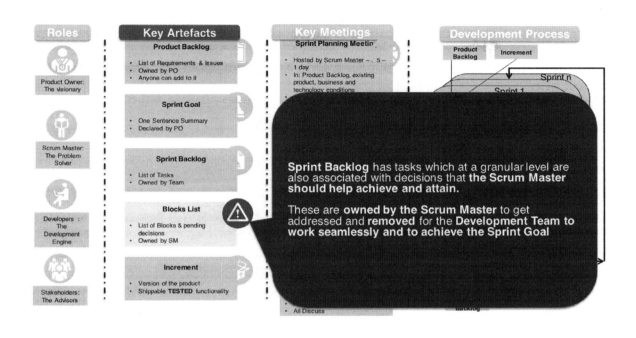

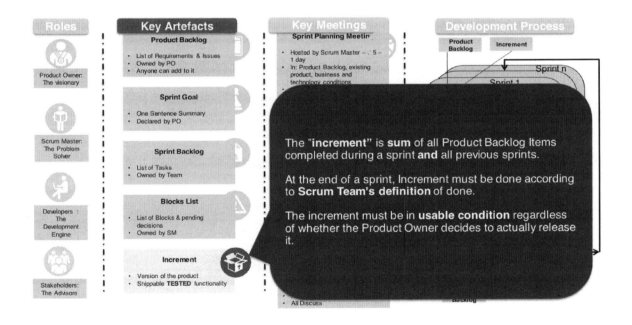

Next, we made sure there is a clear RACI model in place for the different rituals and outputs.

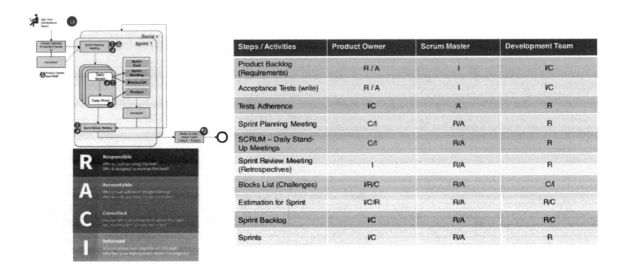

One of the things that establishes a good implementation of Agile is when you account for the Agile steps and stories. Here's a decent way to show case the accounting for Agile that we used:

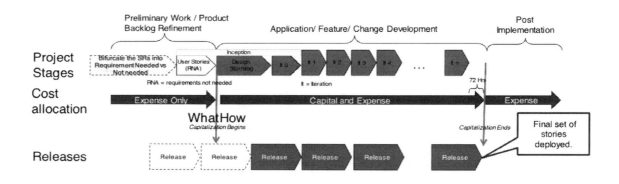

Once you have the set the process, roles, and artefacts are clear, you should next establish the process understanding.

The below image is an example of what I use to explain SCRUM.

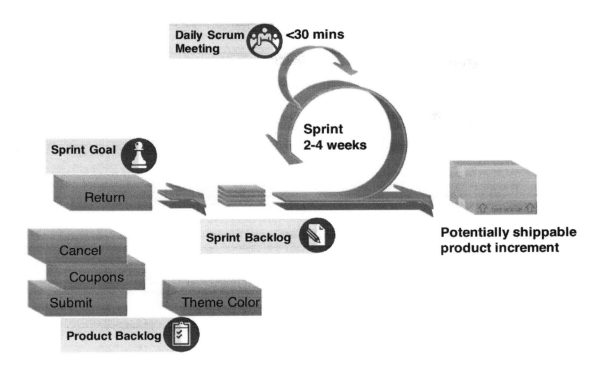

To give you a view and explanation of each of the ritual here is a brief of the steps:

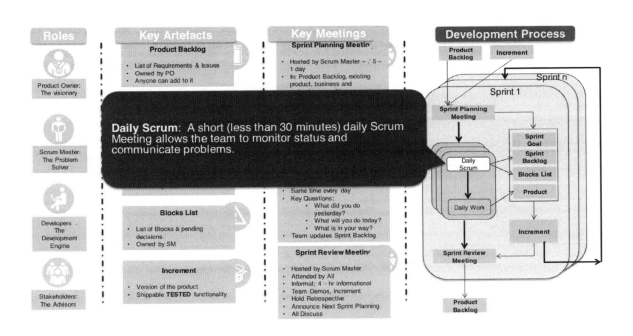

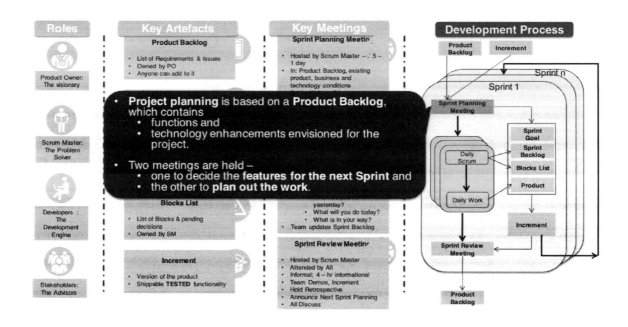

Now that we understand a lot of the new things that we are introducing along the lines of process – SCRUM, people – the new roles, Technology – JIRA Board, etc, and Information – Communication Strategy. We should also focus what the journey should look like and what we have to achieve to reach where Agile is part of the DNA of the organization.

The below image will try and showcase the entire journey scope and where we would want to be:

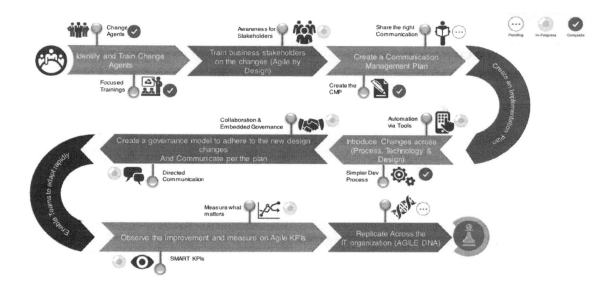

The implementation plan has a bigger vision than just agile, like we stated it is a culture change and the change in the way we wanted to structure the new organization that attracts better work, improves capabilities, and the attached outcomes in the define phase.

Here's the Agile Enterprise Framework for your quick reference that I have put together for your use and understanding:

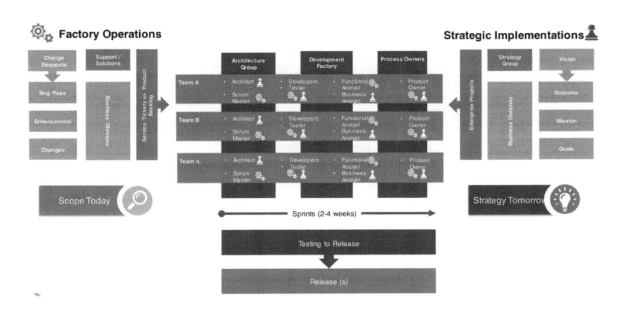

The agile and the factory will work together to achieve a faster, better, and shippable product that is mapped to product owner's need and to the satisfaction of the quality parameters.

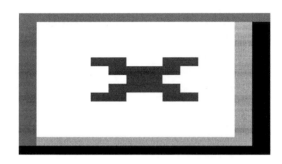

Now as we mapped the current state before implementation begun for the customer journey of the Agile where stakeholders and developers were our customers, here's what the transition state looked like:

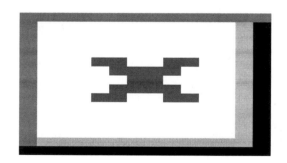

EXTERNAL BENCHMARKING FOR MATURITY MODEL:

In addition to this it is important to also understand the maturity model so that you can assess the improving structure over time.

Here we have leveraged an industry driven maturity model to achieve Agility as below:

PRACTICE	Build Management & Continuous Integration	Environments & Deployments	Release Management & Compliance	Testing	Data Management
Level 3 – Optimizing : Focus on process improvement	Teams regularly meet to discuss integration problems and resolve them with automation, faster feedback, and better visibility	All environments managed effectively. Provisioning fully automated. Virtualization used where applicable	Operations and Delivery teams regularly collaborate to manage risks to reduce cycle time	Production rollbacks are rare. Defects found and fixed immediately	Release to release feedback loop of DB performance and deployment process.
Level 2 – Quantitatively Managed : Process measured and controlled	Build metrics gathered, made visible, and acted on. Builds are nt left broken	Orchestrated deployments managed. Release rollback processes tested	Environments and application health monitored and proactively managed. Cycle Time monitored.	Quality metrics and trends tracked. Non Functional Requirements defined and measured.	Database upgrades and rollbacks tested with every deployment. Database performance monitored and optimized.
Level 1 – Consistent : Automated processes applied across whole application lifecycle	Automated build and test cycle every time a change is committed. Dependencies managed. Re use of scripts and tools.	Fully automated, self service push button process for deploying software. Same process to deploy to evert environment.	Change management and approvals processes defined and enforced. Regulatory and Compliances conditions met	Automated unit and acceptance tests, the latter written with testers. Testing part of development process.	Database changes performed automatically as part of the deployment process
Level 0 – Repeatable : Process documented and partly documented	Regular automated build and testing. Any build can be re created from source control using automated process	Automated deployment to some environments. Creation of new environments is cheap. All configuration externalized / versioned	Painful and infrequent, but reliable, releases. Limited traceability from requirements to release.	Automated tests written as part of story development.	Changes to databases done with automated scripts versioned with applications
Level – 1 – Regressive : Processes unrepeatable, poorly controlled, and reactive	Manual processes building software. No management of artefacts and reports	Manual process for deploying software. Environment specific, binaries. Environments provisioned manually.	Infrequent and unreliable releases.	Manual testing after development	Data migrations un versioned and performed manually

[2]

We then started with the communication strategy implementation. Here's a quick snapshot of what we laid out as a plan:

The image below is indicative of what do we communicate to what sort of stakeholders.

---

[2] Source: Thoughtworks

COMMUNICATION STRATEGY:

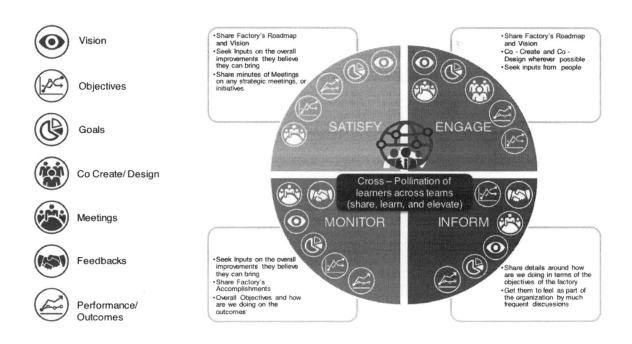

TECHNOLOGY MAPPING:

Next, we address the technology needs, as below:

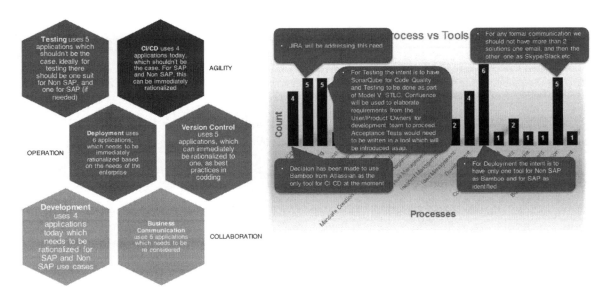

PROCESS MANAGEMENT:

We then address the process, and describe the best of what and how we can eliminate waste from the value stream.

Do zoom in on the images to read more on what was identified and what suggestions did we make to introduce automations where we can.

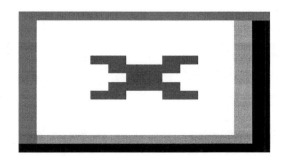

In terms of the communication plan we also put together a very detailed communication plan based on the analysis.

A sample snapshot of the same is illustrated below:

3 COMMUNICATION PLANS

3.1 COMMUNICATIONS MATRIX

The information and the communication logs and artifacts would need to be catalogued and saved for quick references as and when needed. This would improve transparency, intent of the management and help in building trust across teams and awareness on dependencies if any.

Vehicle	Target	Description Purpose	Frequency	Owner	Distribution Vehicle	Internal/ External	Comments
Status Report	All Stakeholders	One page communication of project progress and deliverable status	Weekly	Factory Manager	Email, ECM Solution (Enterprise Content Management)	Internal	
Factory's Goal	All Stakeholders	Factory's Vision, Goal and Objectives to be printed on a banner and posted on the production floor for everyone to understand and be aligned.	NA	Factory	On the production floor walls	Internal	
Agile Dashboards, and SCRUM planning Meeting Boards	Agile Teams / Project Teams	The intent is to have the floor, and the meeting rooms equipped with Chart Papers, and Sticky Notes to be able to conduct quick SCRUM meetings and Daily StandUps	Daily / As Needed	Factory Team	Chart Papers, JIRA, Slack, START, Emails	Internal	

3.1.1 Daily Stand - Up Meetings

The information and captured daily stand up meeting notes and information should also be stored and catalogued where we can. This would improve traceability and help as a reference artifact.

Meeting	Description Purpose	Frequency	Owner	Internal/ External	Comments/ Participants

PROJECT PLAN:

To ensure that this work is done and the entire moving pieces are well addressed we need to have a clear WBS (work breakdown structure), and for the same, here is what we had in place:

Week of	Date	Phase	Activities	Approximate Hrs	Actual Hrs	Workshop Host	Outputs and Notes
18-May	18-May	Define				Jai Vishwakarma	
			§ Conduct Stakeholder identification and analysis	4.00	6.00		Workshop conducted successfully with outcomes, objectives, and KPIs identified. Stakeholders need to be interviewed and scored as a next step
			§ Follow up meeting post WorkShop on Information captured	2.00	2.00		On 21st June, showcased the findings and identified the action items for us
			§ Identify and define the challenges preventing the Agile transformation (Geo, Mindset etc)	12.00			
			§ Capture the Case for Agile Transformation and Design Thinking needs – Product and User Experience Focus	4.00			
				22.00	8.00		
12-Jun		Analyze					
			§ Analyze challenges across – People, Process, and Technology	10.00			
			§ Readiness for Agile Transformation	4.00			This will be a scorecard as identified by Agile and we will be rating the readiness across the dimensions with the stakeholders in person.
			§ Available tools and techniques	2.00			This is the list and inventory of the CI/CD tools, Collaboration Tools, Knowledge Management Tools and others, to see how we leverage them today, and where we lack
			§ Available people, skills and "will" for change	4.00			
			§ Assess the teams and stakeholders on Stakeholder "Influence" scale to get the right buy in for change.	10.00			
				30.00	0.00		
26-Jun		Design					
			§ Leverage CoE and its current design	2.00			Understand detailed tasks and activities as performed by the current CoE, per the charter to gauge the overlap and influence we can positively bring for the change
			§ Align the Agile Transformation Roadmap with the CoE closely to accelerate	2.00			
			§ Design the Agile Team, Suggest the right sizing of the teams, Span and Control, Define the roles.	10.00			
			§ Identify the right skills, and questionnaire for assessing the agile teams, and roles	10.00			
			§ Design the - Design Thinking process, for User Experience	16.00			
				40.00	0.00		
3-Jul		Implement					
			§ Implement Design Thinking Process	8.00			
			§ Implement the Agile Design Methodology**	8.00			
			§ Establish the roles and teams for Agile	4.00			
			§ Train people on Agile and Design Thinking	4.00			
			§ Implement the tools and techniques for Agile Use cases	4.00			
			§ Create a Community of Practitioners (Catalysts) for Agile and Design Thinkers	2.00			
				30.00	0.00		
17-Jul		Govern					
			§Scorecard –embedded with CoE's				
			§Conduct feedback activities	1.00			
			§Governance Model for Continuous Checks	1.00			
			§Community of Practitioners to take governance roles				
			§Business and IT to gauge "tangible" progress	1.00			
			§Methodology adherence	1.00			
			§ External and Internal Audits to be to planned				
				4.00	0.00		
			Total Hrs	126.00			
			TOTAL (Hours)				

Do note that this is a good structure to have as you would need sign off and definition of done in place for stakeholders to confirm if the stage has been accomplished and they have the re-usable assets for repeating this organization re-design process.

As a final output of this exercise we need to have a simple governance process defined.

GOVERNANCE PROCESS:

Remember this is AGILE? And hence the governance process cannot be an overkill, where we are trying to make things leaners, and faster.

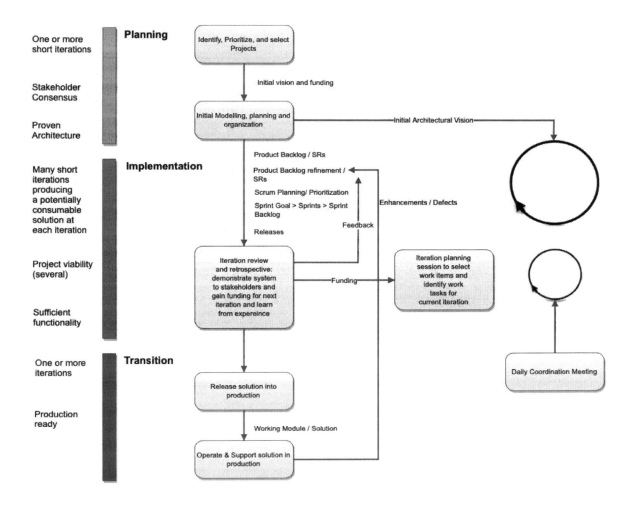

The governance process has to cater and enable the product development vision, and the culture change has to be maintained, and only move upwards for a successful end game.

As a final note we will measure the movement of the As Is and To Be state of the enterprise.

Below image illustrates the roadmap of the organization re-design and what will be expected to come across the dimensions of the organization's agile transformation needs.

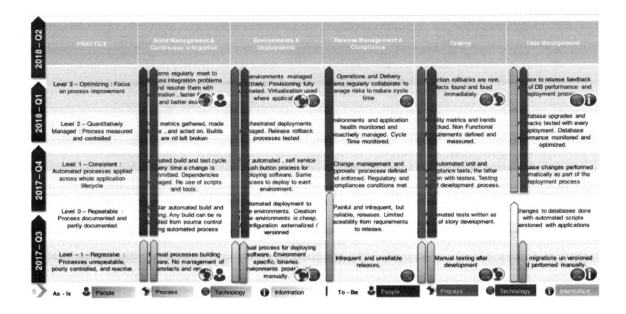

Finally, we are all set to share this knowledge and the artefacts on request to the publisher or the author.

We are glad to share that this is a proven methodology now, and the enterprise has shown a considerable decrease in development time, rise in customer satisfaction, rise in engaged teams, and yes most importantly decrease in bottom line expenses, whereby helping organizations achieve more.

Let me know when you are good to go, and do share your learnings. Remember I am not a guru, but a doer, and believe that not all of the above phases or tools/templates will be of your use, but yes this is a practical implementation of the experiential knowledge and on ground learnings.

Keep innovating, keep learning, stay curious, and stay on ground.

69

Printed in Poland
by Amazon Fulfillment
Poland Sp. z o.o., Wrocław